# the cat intelligence test

# E.M. BARD

# the cat intelligence test

DRAWINGS BY
ROBERT LEYDENFROST

ANGUS & ROBERTSON PUBLISHERS

ANGUS & ROBERTSON PUBLISHERS
London • Sydney • Melbourne

First published by Doubleday & Company, Inc., U.S.A.
First published in Australia by Angus & Robertson Publishers, Australia, 1982
First Published in the United Kingdom
by Angus & Robertson (UK) Ltd 1982
Reprinted 1983, 1984
This edition 1985

©text, E.M. Bard 1980
©illustrations, Doubleday & Company, Inc. 1980

National Library of Australia
Cataloguing-in-publication data.

Bard, E.M.
    The cat intelligence test.

    First published as: The cat I.Q. test. Garden City,
    N.Y.: Doubleday, 1980.
    ISBN 0 207 14327 7.

    1. Cats — Psychology — Anecdotes, facetiae, satire, etc.
    2. Animal intelligence — Anecdotes, facetiae, satire,
    etc. I. Title.

156'.39'0207

Printed in the United Kingdom

# Contents

# INTRODUCTION

Anyone who has ever owned a cat has at one time or another been amazed at his pet's natural abilities and wisdom. At times, cats and kittens seem to thrive on entertaining their owners with cute tricks and unusual behavior. In actuality, the cantankerous and often irrepressible behavior is an important part of their intellectual development.

Cats develop their learning and understanding ability according to their background, their experiences, their age, and their living conditions. Your pet may be around conditions that make him* nervous or upset. He may be around conditions that make him relaxed and lazy. Sometimes, when they are bothered, cats try to run and hide. Sometimes they will attempt to fight or outsmart whatever is bothering them. The way in which your pet responds to his living conditions is an indication of his learning and understanding ability, or, simply put, his intelligence.

The Cat I.Q. Test measures the overall intellectual development of your cat. There are four areas of development that, when taken together, make up your cat's intelligence:

**1.   Coordination Skills**—This includes the use of small and large muscles, how your cat moves and balances, his reflex actions, body sensitivity and control, and his preference for using one side of his body over another.

**2.   Communication Skills**—This area of cat development deals with the pet's ability to make himself understood or to get attention. Cats are able to gain attention by using both their voices and their bodies. Communication skills measured here include voice level and intensity, and your cat's ability to understand directions.

* Note: "Him" is used throughout as the neuter pronoun, and of course includes "her" as well.

**3. Reasoning Ability**—This is perhaps the most difficult area to measure. It involves testing how your cat solves the various problems he encounters and how he adjusts to his surroundings. Your cat's alertness, concentration, and reactions to dangerous situations are also measured.

**4. Social Behavior**—This includes a wide range of both personal and social skills that are developed and used by your cat. The way in which your cat gets along with you, other people, and other animals is an important indication of your cat's overall intelligence.

The Cat I.Q. Test is divided into four sections, three of which involve observing your cat in a variety of usual situations. After you have carefully watched your cat in these situations a number of times, you should mark down how he behaved, either where provided for in each section or on the scorecard on page 94.

Section B of the test is an administered test. For this section, you perform certain activities with your cat and mark down your cat's response. Since the cat must actively participate in the test to score well on this section, it is important that you provide him with the specific testing items mentioned in the directions to that section. You'll find that they are common objects. Also, you should only administer this section of the test when your cat is calm and cooperative. (The test may, of course, be discontinued at any time, and started over later.)

The Cat I.Q. Test may be used for all cats or kittens. It is recommended that the pet be at least eight weeks old before the test is attempted. Although the test may be given more than once, a one-day waiting period is suggested in order to avoid the practice effect often found in a retesting situation. Careful administration of the test is necessary in order to obtain a good estimate of the pet's intellectual abilities. Do not teach your cat the correct responses. The goal of this test is to observe and record the total way in which your pet has been able to adjust to his surroundings. By using several of the major areas of pet development to judge the cat's learning and understanding skills, you will be obtaining his overall intellectual level. No precoaching or remedial drill may be provided before the test is given.

When testing handicapped cats, special provisions need to be made. If the pet has a visual or hearing problem, award the pet credit for items he is unable to attempt due to his learning disability. Physically disabling conditions should be handled in the same manner.

After you have done all the testing and have determined your cat's final score, you can compare his score to that of other cats in general, or to those of your cat's type, sex, or age. Of course, keep in mind that intelligence is only one facet of your cat's unique personality. Some wonderful pets may score poorly on this test because of limited experience or unusual backgrounds. This book provides specific suggestions for improving your cat's intelligence and sociability. But for now, you're ready to begin.

# THE CAT INTELLIGENCE TEST

## SECTION A: CAT OBSERVATION TEST

**Directions**
Read each of the test questions carefully. Rate your pet according to the scale below. Before rating your cat, observe him in a variety of situations and at different times. This will provide a more accurate measure.

**Rating Scale**
The following scale should be referred to when scoring your pet's behavior:

| Category | Rating Points |
|---|---|
| Never | 1 |
| Seldom | 2 |
| Usually | 3 |
| Very Frequently | 4 |
| Always | 5 |

**Recording**
Place the appropriate rating point on the line following the test item or on the scorecard on page 94. This will be the number of points your pet receives for each item.

**Scoring**
At the end of Section A, add up the total number of points earned.

**Points
Received**

1.  Eats or requests food on a regular schedule
    (e.g., desire for food can be predicted, eats
    around the same time each day).

———————

2.  Enjoys a variety of foods (e.g., both pet food
    and people food).

    _____

3.  Is able to show displeasure with food he is
    given (e.g., turns dish over, uses dish for litter
    box).                                             _____

4. Cleans face after eating (e.g., wipes whiskers or mouth with tongue or paws). _____

5.  Keeps tail flat on floor when eating (tail touches
    floor behind or to side of pet).                    _____

6.  Is able to get the attention of people around
    him when he wants (e.g., by rubbing, clawing,
    purring, crying).                                      _____

7.  Recognizes sounds that precede his feeding
    (e.g., can opener, refrigerator door, food
    wrapper).

    _4_

8.  Sleeps in the same place each night.    _____

**9.** Moves ears while sleeping in response to noises
in his surroundings (e.g., phone ringing,
doorbell, water running, door closing, voices,
wind, rain).

_____

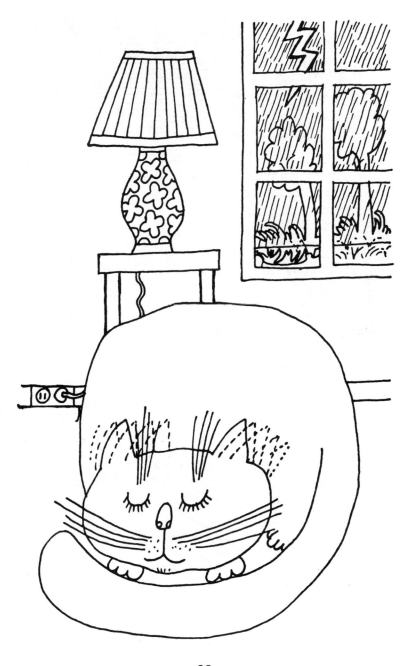

10. Has regularly established sleeping patterns
    (goes to sleep and gets up around the same
    times each day).                                            _____

11.  Watches movement around him (e.g., sits by
     window, observes other animals, is sensitive to
     small movements).                                    _____

12. Reveals his mood through the position or
state of his tail (e.g., bushy, hidden, wrapped
around legs, curled around body, straight up in
air, limp or relaxed).                                    —————

13.   Is able to remain totally still, while awake, for
      a minimum of 120 seconds (two minutes).

_____

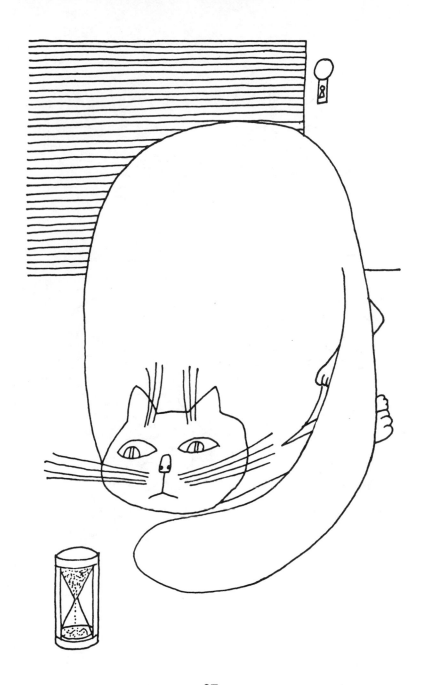

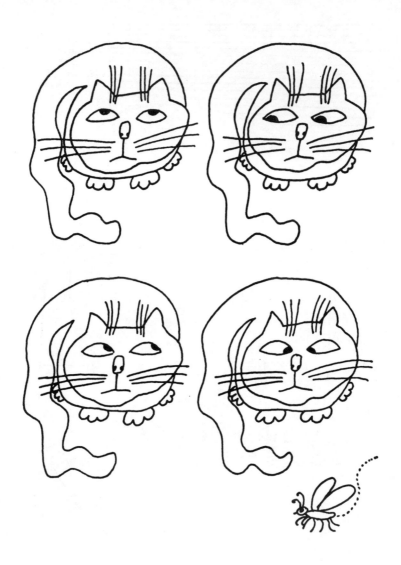

14. Is able to watch moving objects with his eyes only, without moving his body (is aware of movement but keeps body rigid and still). _____

**15.** Shows awareness of odors in his immediate
surroundings (either likes or dislikes the smell of
perfumes, lotions, medicines, foods, animals,
etc.).

_____

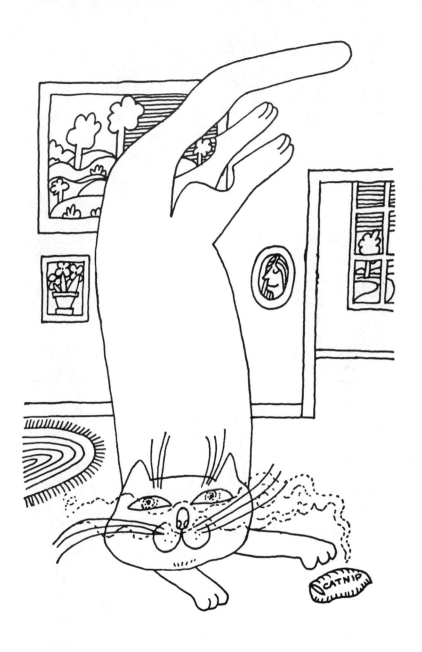

16. Makes various sounds to request different needs
(specific cries for hunger, injury, pain, attention,
pleasure, etc.).                                    _____

17. Shows or displays his feelings toward other animals or persons in his household (e.g., jealousy, love, worry).

_____

18. Has preference for certain animals (e.g., plays
with certain animals, enjoys the presence of
other animals, likes to watch animals on
television).

_____

19. Favors one front paw over the other and uses
    this favorite paw for various activities (e.g.,
    washing face, playing with toys, grasping
    objects).                                          4

20.  Shows preference for specific objects (e.g.,
     favorite pillow, toy, blanket).

**21.** Enjoys being touched around neck, face, and
back (especially stroking or petting).

_____

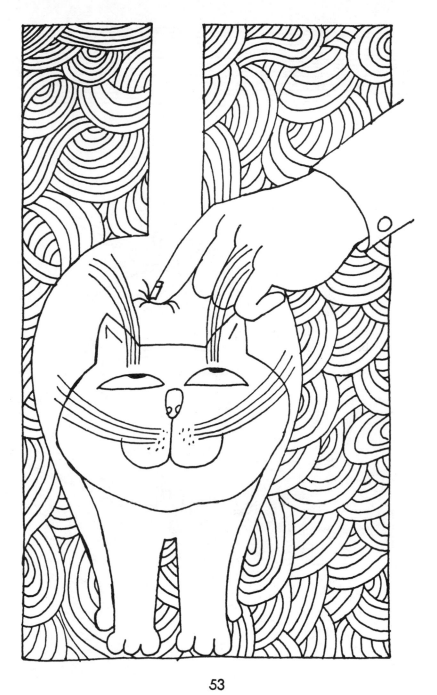

22. Sits on or near adults and makes sounds
showing pleasure (e.g., purring, cooing,
gurgling).

**23.** Reacts to music and rhythm (e.g., sitting on
radio or piano; moving in time to the music by
rocking, dancing, twitching tail).                    _____

24. Is aware of the passing of time (e.g., can
predict or anticipate when certain persons will
return home, or leave home).                    _____

**25.** Can predict change in the weather that will
take place within one week (e.g., hides before
storm comes, stays close to fireplace before
severe cold arrives, seems to know when
unusual weather is approaching).                    _____

**Total Points Section A:**   _____

# SECTION B: CAT PERFORMANCE TEST

**Materials Needed**
1. Shoestring or thick yarn, approximately thirty inches long
2. Small ball made of plastic, wood, or rubber
3. Pencil (use eraser end or an unsharpened pencil)
4. Feather or thick rubber band
5. Bell, or butter knife and small drinking glass

**Directions**
Gather the testing materials needed for this section. Then perform each of the activities listed up to five times to obtain the best possible response.

Before administering the test, make sure your cat is calm, cooperative, and in a good mood. If he becomes tired, disinterested, nervous, or uncooperative, or leaves the testing area, this part of the test should be stopped until the cat is more comfortable.

**Recording**
Make a check mark next to each response given by your pet, here or on the scorecard on page 94. Performance items may have more than one check mark. Some performance items may have no check marks.

**Scoring**
Add up the total number of points earned. Record this total at the end of Section B. No credit is given if the pet continually runs away, ignores the testing session, or refuses to respond.

**Testing Time**
Section B usually takes about fifteen minutes. This time will vary depending on how cooperative your cat is.

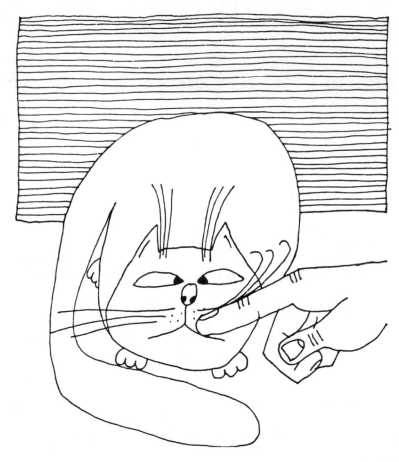

1. Touch or stroke your cat lightly and gently around
the mouth area with your finger:
   Closes eyes: ⎯⎯⎯ 1 point
   Shakes head: ⎯⎯⎯ 1 point
   Licks mouth: ⎯⎯⎯ 2 points ⎯⎯⎯

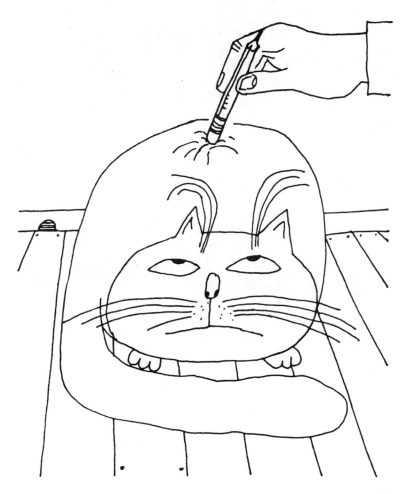

2. Touch your cat gently on his back with your
   finger or the pencil:
   Ripples or moves back
       fur:                   _____  1 point
   Shakes fur:          _____  1 point
   Licks spot touched:   _____  2 points    _____

**3.** Touch the inside hair of either of your cat's ears
very lightly with your finger or pencil:

Shakes entire head: _____ 1 point

Twitches the ear: _____ 2 points

Rubs or touches ear with
    paw: _____ 2 points   _____

4. Ring the bell or tap a glass with a butter knife to
   make a soft ringing noise behind your cat:
   Moves or twitches ear(s): _____ 1 point
   Turns head partly around: _____ 1 point
   Turns head completely
      around to area where
      sound came from: _____ 2 points      _____

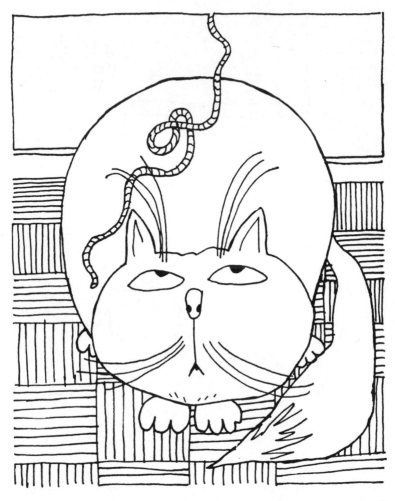

**5.** Place the string or yarn on your cat's back. Be
careful not to let the string hang down and touch
the floor. Completely let go of string:
Ripples or moves fur: _____ 1 point
Removes string in any way: _____ 2 points _____

6. Pull the string or yarn slowly across the floor in
   front of your cat:
   Watches with eyes:     _____   1 point
   Touches with nose:     _____   1 point
   Grabs with paw(s):     _____   2 points     _____

**7.** Place the feather or thick rubber band on the
floor two to four inches in front of your cat:

| | | |
|---|---|---|
| Touches with paw(s): | _____ | 1 point |
| Touches with nose: | _____ | 1 point |
| Begins to chew feather or rubber band: | _____ | 1 point |
| Picks up feather or rubber band with paw: | _____ | 2 points |
| Transfers feather or rubber band from paw to paw: | _____ | 2 points _____ |

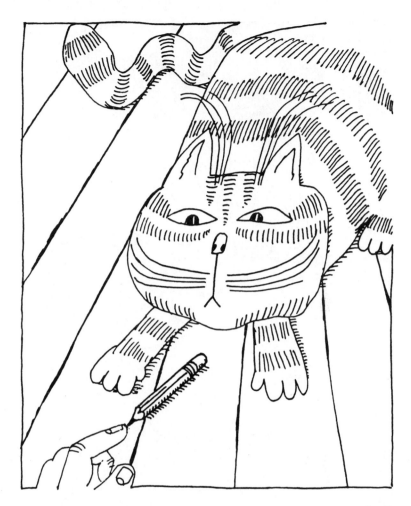

**8.** Slowly move the pencil along the floor toward
your cat:

Touches pencil with paw(s): _____ 1 point

Touches pencil with same
paw two or more times: _____ 2 points _____

9.  Roll the ball on the floor toward your cat:

    | | | |
    |---|---|---|
    | Touches with paw(s): | _____ | 1 point |
    | Touches with nose: | _____ | 1 point |
    | Begins to play with ball: | _____ | 2 points |

    _____

**Total Points Section B:** _____

# SECTION C: EXTRA CREDIT

**Directions**
Read each of the following statements to determine if your pet qualifies for these bonus points.

**Recording**
Enter the number of bonus points earned to the right of each item. Partial credit is not permitted.

**Scoring**
At the end of Section C, add up the total number of points your pet has received.

1.  Is able to make sounds *upon request* (4 bonus
    points).

    _____

**2.** Can sit, stand, or roll over *upon request* (4 bonus
points).  _____

3.  Is able to pass any item from paw to paw or hit
    it back and forth in the air (4 bonus points).                    _____

**Points
Earned**

**4.** Has learned to use the people's toilet instead of
a litter box (4 bonus points).

_____

**Points
Earned**

**5.** Is able to balance on hind legs for at least five
seconds (2 bonus points).

_____

78

Points
Earned

6.  Has learned to walk on hind legs for at least five
    steps (4 bonus points).                                    _____

                          **Total Number of Bonus Points:**    _____

# SECTION D: CREDIT DEDUCTIONS

**Directions**
Read each of the following statements to determine if points should be taken away from your cat's score.

**Recording**
Place the number of deducted points to the right of each item. Partial deductions are not permitted.

**Scoring**
Add up the total number of point deductions. Record this total at the end of Section D.

Points
Taken Away

1. Continually runs into walls or doors (deduct
   1 point).

_____

**2.** Goes to sleep on a ledge and falls off while
sleeping (deduct 1 point).

_____

**3.** Constantly sits, stands, steps, or sleeps in his
food dish (deduct 1 point).

_____

4. Wakes up from nap, stretches, then goes back
   to sleep sitting or standing up (deduct 1 point).

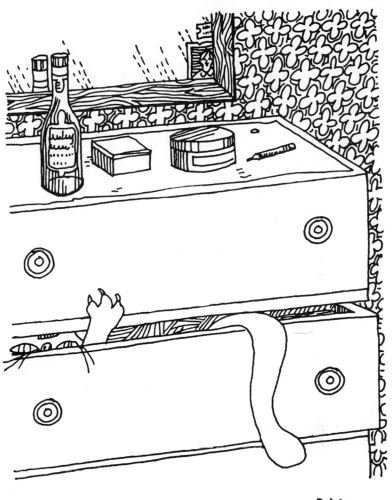

**Points
Taken Away**

5.  Goes to sleep in closet or drawer and ends up
    trapped inside (deduct 1 point).

6. Jumps onto toilet when seat is up and falls
   in (deduct 1 point).

———

**Total Number of Points Deducted:** ————

# SCORING THE CAT I.Q. TEST

**Step 1:**
Double the number of points earned in Section B. Now add to this the number of points for Sections A and C.

Section A=                                 points    _93_

Section B×2=                            points    _____

Section C=                                 points    _2_

**Total points earned from Sections A+(B×2)+C=**    _____

**Step 2:**
Record any points listed in Section D.
Section D=                      points to subtract    _____

**Step 3:**
Obtain the Total Test Score by subtracting any points recorded in Step 2 from the points recorded in Step 1.

**Total Test Score: [A+(B×2)+C] − D=**    _____

**Step 4:**
Use this Total Test Score when referring to the Cat I.Q. Classification Chart below. Now you can know how smart your cat is—really!

# CAT I.Q. CLASSIFICATION CHART

| Total Test Score | Classification |
|---|---|
| 60–69 | **Below Normal** |
| 70–89 | **Low Normal** |
| 90–109 | **Normal** |
| 110–119 | **Above Normal** |
| 120–139 | **Superior** |
| 140 and above | **Genius** |

# ANALYZING YOUR CAT'S PERFORMANCE

Your cat's score on The Cat I.Q. Test should give you some idea of his intellectual development at the present time. It will also give you an idea of how your cat's learning skills and understanding ability compare to those of other cats. Many factors influence this score, such as the cat's age, background, and experience. A young kitten, for example, may score better as it matures. Other factors are in your control, and later on there will be some suggestions on how you can improve your cat's performance.

This section will provide you with definitions of each of the categories on the Classification Chart. By reading about your cat's category, you will gain a greater understanding of your cat's abilities and needs.

### Genius Range
Cats with a score of 140 or more are gifted and extremely bright. They are able to function well socially and exhibit exceptional reasoning skills. Extremely well developed coordination and balance have been demonstrated. They communicate well and often develop strong and distinct relationships with their owners. Without a doubt, these cats are quite creative and original in the ways they cope with their daily lives. These pets are often very attractive, mature, healthy, and stable.

### Superior Range
Pets that are grouped within the 120 to 139 point range are usually quite clever and able to grasp new information quickly. These pets are highly intelligent and easily gain the attention and approval of their owners. Pets within this category are well coordinated and have good muscle development and posture. They are usually mature and can adjust quickly to changing situations. They have learned to get along smoothly with their owners and family and have mastered the skills they need to survive.

### Above Normal Range
Cats that scored between 110 and 119 points have demonstrated good intellectual ability. These pets display common sense, strong social skills,

88

and a better than average ability to communicate. Cats that fall within this range are cooperative and friendly, physically well developed, and able to cope with most frustrations.

### Normal Range
Cats that are grouped within the 90 to 109 point range are well liked by their owners and are able to cope with the usual demands made upon them. A sufficient amount of communication between pet and owner exists for a good relationship. Coordination is also satisfactory. These cats are sociable and have developed adequate ways of coping with life's daily frustrations.

### Low Normal Range
Cats whose scores fall within the 70 to 89 point range may need extra time or experience to realize their potential. These pets are usually friendly and tend to be adjusted to their surroundings. They are able to function quite well in spite of possible minor weaknesses in communication, coordination, or social behavior. These pets often improve their scores when they are older or more mature.

### Below Normal Range
Pets that are classified in the 60 to 69 point range appear to be in need of special assistance; otherwise, they may encounter some difficulties coping with their daily routine. Lack of experience, lack of attention, or lack of the right type of surroundings may have contributed to their weak performances. Additional time and care will often lead to considerable improvement.

## HOW TO IMPROVE YOUR CAT'S I.Q.

Your cat's score on The Cat I.Q. Test is not just the result of his own abilities. Many factors influence his performance: his age, his background, and his experience, for example. Some of these factors are in your control. The following techniques should increase your cat's intelligence and happiness, regardless of how well he did on the test.

1. Encourage your cat's natural (and infinite) curiosity. Present your pet with new and novel toys and equipment and even food (though don't overfeed him). Praise your cat for his attempts to approach new things.

2. Set aside a specific amount of time each day to talk and play with your pet. Even the most sober cat can become as playful as he was as a kitten, if you spark his interest.

3. Keep your voice level pleasing and comforting. Cats respond quickly to the voice level of those around them.

4. Reward your cat immediately for good behavior. Do not delay, as this will confuse him. Rewards such as a favorite toy, special food, or a gentle petting may be given.

5. Promote a healthy and stable relationship with your pet through physical contact such as brushing, combing, or rubbing your cat daily. This will help develop and promote feelings of security and foster a high level of emotional stability.

6. Make your pet feel important and needed by praising him for the things he does well. Provide opportunities for him to repeat that activity and encourage him to do so Don't frustrate your cat by demanding or expecting him to do things he can't.

7. Be consistent when enforcing rules of conduct. Make sure your cat knows what type of behavior is expected from him. If he consistently behaves incorrectly in certain situations, set up a mock situation to provoke the behavior (for example, set the table for dinner and wait for your cat to jump up) and then discipline the cat immediately. Punishment should always be immediate and firm, but gentle.

8. Eliminate the teasing or tormenting situations your pet encounters. Make sure that children know not to pull a cat's tail, for example. Try to provide only a minimal amount of physical and emotional stress.

9. Be sensitive to the needs of your cat. However, do not let him manipulate you. A relationship of mutual trust and admiration is necessary to foster both intelligence and happiness.

# COMPARATIVE SCORES BY AGE, SEX AND TYPE

The tables on the following pages compare the performances of cats of various ages, sexes, and general types.

Table A depicts the predicted distribution of scores if every cat in the cat population were to take the test.

The scores in tables B, C, and D are based only on a limited and biased sampling of cats. This included only cats held in high esteem by their owners and did not include any neglected, unwanted, homeless, or sick cats. As a result, the scores on tables B, C, and D are significantly higher than they would be if they were based on a random sampling of cats, and no definite conclusions should be drawn from these comparative tables. We do hope, however, that this section provides you with a context for rating your cat's intelligence, as well as being a starting point for future studies.

## Table A

### Predicted Distribution of Scores for All Cats

| Classification Category | Percentage Predicted |
| --- | --- |
| Below Normal Range | 2% |
| Low Normal Range | 14% |
| Normal Range | 68% |
| Above Normal Range | 14% |
| Superior Range | 2% |
| Genius Range | .02% |

## Table B

### Scores by Age

| Age* | Mean Score |
| --- | --- |
| 8 months to 3 years | 108 |
| 4 years to 7 years | 133 |
| 8 years to 11 years | 144 |
| 12 years to 15 years | 123 |

* Age should have little influence on the intellectual development of cats, except in the case of a very young, immature, or highly distracted kitten. Once again, these results are based only on a limited and biased sample.

**Table C**

**Scores by Sex**

| Sex* | Mean Score† |
|---|---|
| Male | 140.00 |
| Female | 117.25 |

* Neutered cats were included in the sampling.

† The superior scores of male cats here can be attributed to the high percentage of Siamese males among the male cats tested. This breed scored significantly better than others on the test (see Table D). Since the breed factor corrupted the sex factor here, no definite conclusions about the relative intelligence of male and female cats should be drawn from this sampling.

**Table D**

**Scores by Type**

| General Type* | Mean Score† |
|---|---|
| Long-haired | 121.50 |
| Short-haired | 122.00 |
| Siamese | 140.00 |

* These three general types of cats were listed here, rather than specific breeds, because of the limited number of cats of certain breeds in the norming sample.

† The difference in the scores of long-haired and short-haired cats is not statistically significant. However, Siamese cats did score significantly higher than other types. This can be attributed to the superior communication skills evident in that breed. Siamese cats are often very vocal and expressive.

# SCORECARD

This answer sheet may be used instead of recording the results in the test booklet.

**Section A**   (Observation Scale)

| | | | | |
|---|---|---|---|---|
| 1. __ | 6. __ | 11. __ | 16. __ | 21. __ |
| 2. __ | 7. __ | 12. __ | 17. __ | 22. __ |
| 3. __ | 8. __ | 13. __ | 18. __ | 23. __ |
| 4. __ | 9. __ | 14. __ | 19. __ | 24. __ |
| 5. __ | 10. __ | 15. __ | 20. __ | 25. __ |

SECTION A
TOTAL=. ____

**Section B**   (Performance Scale)

| | | | | | |
|---|---|---|---|---|---|
| 1. closes eyes | __ 1 point | | 6. watches | __ 1 point |
| shakes head | __ 1 point | | touches | __ 1 point |
| licks mouth | __ 2 points | | grabs | __ 2 points |
| 2. ripples | __ 1 point | | 7. paw | __ 1 point |
| shakes | __ 1 point | | nose | __ 1 point |
| licks | __ 2 points | | chews | __ 1 point |
| 3. shakes head | __ 1 point | | picks up | __ 2 points |
| twitches ear | __ 2 points | | transfers | __ 2 points |
| rubs ear | __ 2 points | | 8. paw | __ 1 point |
| 4. moves ears | __ 1 point | | same paw | __ 2 points |
| turns head partly | __ 1 point | | 9. paw | __ 1 point |
| turns head 180° | __ 2 points | | nose | __ 1 point |
| 5. ripples fur | __ 1 point | | plays | __ 2 points |
| removes string | __ 2 points | | | |

SECTION B
TOTAL= ____

**Section C**   (Extra Credit)

| | | |
|---|---|---|
| 1. __ | 3. __ | 5. __ |
| 2. __ | 4. __ | 6. __ |

SECTION C
TOTAL= ____

**Section D**   (Deductions)

| | | |
|---|---|---|
| 1. __ | 3. __ | 5. __ |
| 2. __ | 4. __ | 6. __ |

SECTION D
TOTAL= ____

**Scoring:** A+(B×2)+C—D=TOTAL TEST SCORE: ____